THE ANCIENT GEMSTONE

Volume 1

THE ANCIENT GEMSTONE

Volume 1

SOPHIE PETERSON

Waterside Productions
Cardiff-by-the-Sea, California

Copyright © 2020 by Sophie Peterson
www.theancientgemstone.com

All rights reserved. This book or any portion thereof may not
be reproduced or used in any manner whatsoever without the
express written permission of the publisher except for the use of
brief quotations in articles and book reviews.

Printed in the United States of America

First Printing, 2020

ISBN-13: 978-1-947637-26-9 print edition
ISBN-13: 978-1-947637-27-6 ebook edition

Waterside Productions
2055 Oxford Ave
Cardiff, CA 92007
www.waterside.com

For Aimée

Table of Contents

....

FOREWORD

....

Focus on how to break free,
not what's going to happen afterwards.

LIKE-MINDED CREATURES

Align with like-minded creatures
they'll inspire you to dig deeper

go to the depths of the mind
the bottom of the spine

to find the very well-hidden seeker

1

THE LOSS AND THE LOVE

Everyone is you
seven billion different variations of yourself
in each reflection

within our conflicting ideologies
our large collection of belief systems
we are all connected

because of the natural breath
the loss
and the love

I'VE GOT YOU

I've got you
even if you don't want to be held

I get you
even if you feel misunderstood

I love you
even if you refuse to believe

I hear you
even if you don't want to be loud

I see you
even if you want to be forgotten
in the crowd

I bare it all open
dive into devotion

you won't ever be lost
if I'm found

THE TEACHER

Find the teacher
who will always be available

who will be fair, honest
and will never ask for anything in exchange

who will be forever loyal to your well-being
who will hold your heart gently
and bring you home safely

who will comfort you like a mother
and protect you like a father

who will be your greatest friend
and your most noble partner

who will love you unconditionally
even in your darkest hour

go and find yourself
great teacher

for it is you
you have been waiting for

FLOAT

. . . .

Every night before you close your eyes
release all energy ties

disengage for the moment
float in your circle

enjoy the silence and rest well
when you wake in the morning
you can begin again

THE AMAZON

Many times
the earth has seen the moon rise
the sun set
the ground split in two
the oceans dry
and the rivers flood

many times
the earth has seen the fires catch
the rocks tumble to the sea
and the stars shoot across the sky

many times
the earth has seen the animals run
the wolf cry
the baby born
the joy in our hearts
the tears in our eyes

many times
the earth has seen the future repeat the past
the history of existence expand and retreat

the buildings climb
and the brick crumble to the floor

many times
the earth has felt the movement
of it's nature spread across the land
it's old, it's new

it lies, it's true
it's home to us
to me and you

many times
the earth has turned getting wiser
and younger while we've watched
thinking there's something we could do

to stop it
to accelerate it
to control it
and to manipulate it

hold us closer to you great earth
remind us why we breathe

the air in our lungs is the power of your pull
if it's us against the world
then it's us against ourselves

we are the great extension
of your billion year old shell

MY GIFT

If it is my gift to see,
why have I been so blind?

If it is my gift to breathe,
why do I always feel winded?

If it is my gift to receive,
why do I come up short?

If it is my gift to love,
why do I forget to open my heart?

If it is my gift to hear,
why can I not understand?

If my gift is my energy,
when will I forgive my fellow man?

because dear child,
you have been crossed
saddened and let down

but even within your fears
refuse to give up finding your crown

TIMES OF TROUBLE

In times of trouble
when the exploitation of human rights
is combined with an overbearing freedom
of individuality

so free that we have learned
to play our own god
resulting in the dishonor of self
or complete self-actualization

it's helpful to remember
many realities exist as they always have
done whether we understand them or not

for that reason we look
to further our knowledge
not to cure our sadness about the entrapment
of so many minds

but to release ourselves from ignorance
and together rise in joy

The Nothingness

When you engage in the nothingness
it ceases to be nothing
and becomes something

whatever you give your attention to
will develop meaning
you'll find a way to make it comprehendible
part of you

for a moment
or a lifetime

You

. . . .

When you feel stripped of who you are
ask the stars to guide you

the moon to hold you
and the earth to ground you

ask the ocean to cleanse you
the fruits to detox you
and the sacred connection to activate you

ask the yoga to stretch you
the singing to release you
the sleep to recharge you
and give the service that remains in you

THEM

. . . .

Love as if it's the last time you'll see them
it changes the perspective immediately

the idea of never holding them again
is so painful
you fast-forward through all the trauma
and come to them

finally getting to the real reason why you
care about this life,
it's for the people you love

which means it's on you
to show up for yourself no matter what

for the people who can't love themselves
who don't love themselves

who can't apologize
who don't apologize

who can't take accountability
who won't take accountability

who can't love you like you need them to
who don't love you like you want them to

show up anyway
because you already know the life of turning
away
but you also know life afterwards

where you are capable and strong enough
to love them regardless
and face everything as a reflection

we all need one more person in our corner
to be that shining glimmer of hope
and to love unconditionally

THE KEY

....

You hold the key
to your own brilliant power

your own durable strength
your own phenomenal inner healing

you are capable of anything,
so don't let life use you

don't let this sick system gobble you up
and throw away the key

be aware
of the simple things

eating
speaking

breathing
moving

look after yourself better
love yourself better

keep going
even when everyone else around you
might be giving up

THERE WILL BE VOICES

There will be voices
which inspire you
frighten you

lift you up
bring you down

guide you
misdirect you

love you
and hate you

choose wisely
what you decide to listen to

Have The Conversation

Have the conversation
speak what you deserve into existence

the next move
is to live what you preach

adjust accordingly and be self-taught
there is an amazing world you can create
for yourself

it's available to you
be honest with what you need

feel it with your heart
be committed

make the best of it
and gratitude will set you apart

THE REASON
YOU ARE HERE

Decide what kind of day you are going to have
do not stop to partake in thing's that are
beneath you

keep your positive momentum going
moving on and letting go
appears hard initially

because you feel as if you don't deserve
what's best for you
if what you love is being taken away
and causing hurt

how can it be what you really need
if the result is more pain

we're systemically geared not to embrace
change when it's difficult
we only embrace change
when it make us happy

so don't stop because it's uncomfortable
change how you feel about life changing

when you are awake
you get to be reborn every moment

everyday you can start again
and make new choices

that pull you closer
to the reason you are here

LETTING GO

When you grasp too tight

You're not paying attention
to what you're holding onto

you're only paying attention
to not letting go

Within Our Solitude

Even within our solitude
we are destined to live here altogether

if you look down
you'll never survive

if you look up
they'll eat you alive

if you look straight ahead
you'll open your eyes

fill your cup
give your service

name your price
honor your life

live your word
and speak your truth

SEPARATION OF SELF

Depression is an awakening
it's the indication of separation of self

the warning signal of disconnection
from within

witnessing the divide amongst people
feeling the divorce within love

depression is when you ignore the body
and let the busy mind take over

if you are hurting
there is opportunity to heal

your happiness lies in your hands
life is here for you
not against you

depression is when you refuse to look
at what's hindering your well-being

so go to the mirror
the eyes never lie

you'll know what you need
don't dwell

just see
and set it free

WE MOVE LIKE THE WEATHER

....

The earth has been turning long before us
and it will keep on turning long after us

whatever you feel in this moment isn't
permanent
relationships end and new ones start

your sadness is temporary
just like your happiness
so be present

we move like the weather
we mirror the earth's transition
pulling away
and then coming home to itself again

renewing and shedding
becoming and undoing

we know we are alive
but how are we living

we are not above the ebb and flow
life is not a race but a dance

your value lies in how you treat others
and how you treat yourself
not how productive you can be

we're all so lost in doing
and not being

so what are you doing
and how are you being?

ENERGY

....

We all remember things differently

what is true for you
may not be true for someone else

what's true for someone else
may not be true for you

but there is one truth
that is true for all

which is energy

light consciousness
that thing we're all made from

it takes having faith
in something you can't necessarily see
or hear

but you can feel
loud and clear

Our Holy Book

Our body is our holy book
our record keeper

our sundial
our treasure map
our spirit teacher

constantly conducting trauma analysis
to aid us in neutralizing emotional toxicity

our body speaks to us
if we create space for stillness we can hear
the messages

Parts Of You

. . . .

There are parts of you
that don't live in the light

so you have to bring the light
to them instead

As You Revolutionize

As you revolutionize
you come to understand

that feeling low
doesn't mean you have to get high

that the healthiest you've ever looked
isn't necessarily the best you've ever felt

that having wealth
doesn't make you rich with wisdom

and being angry
definitely won't make you feel love

When You Teach About Light

When you teach about light
you address darkness

when you teach about love
you acknowledge pain

you can't know one without the other
because you'd have nothing to compare it to
nothing to identify the difference with

to live in fear is to not trust your instincts
to live in anxiety is to not be comfortable
with the pace of your life

you will get to where you need to be
do it with patience
transcend your being

conquer the hour, the day, the week, the month
by this time next year
you'll be in a completely different space

it's not about where you are
but how you show up

THE WAY

The only way to feel great in a society
which profits from us feeling inadequate
is to go beyond the surface

go down the rabbit hole
until you find wonderland

if you know how deep the corruption
and exploitation runs
within every social structure
you've not distraught for very long

instead you become desperate
to find an alternative path
a different way to live

that's why many turn to enlightenment
it's the way in
to find the way out

Sip Water

When you sip water
sip for those who have little or no access
to clean drink

when you eat
eat for those who have little or no food
to nourish themselves with

when you love
love for those who have been starved from it

when you work
work with honor in your heart for those who
cannot provide

when you practice
practice for all beings on earth

THE FORBIDDEN
KNOWLEDGE

The forbidden knowledge is you
you have the answers to make sense
of this life

the ongoing quest
a thirsty flower waiting for the
high desert rain

you exist
you belong
you are enough

award yourself love
become your expertise

expand your self-awareness
do what leads to growth

OTHER PEOPLE

It's not about other people

how they've misled you
how they've mistreated you
how they've ignored your voice

put words in your mouth
messed up your mind
and made your body feel sick with shame

it's about how you've let that take over
your whole world
remember that it's yours
your beautiful world

rebuild what you've given away
reform what's been stolen from you

FORMER LIVES

There is no identity crisis
the world is constantly changing

you evolve along
in it, with it

your former lives
are all the people you've been in this one

LIBERATION

If this is the work you've here to do
it'll lead to liberation

not confinement
not even by gravity

your people will find you
they will be moved by your ability
to speak to their delicate souls

to mend their broken hearts
to clear their confused minds

so all living beings can have the option
to transition over in peace
rather than in pain

An Incredible Life

Your heart
can take you to the moon

and your mind
can take you to the deepest root
of the oldest tree

your outlook on the world
shows up within all aspects of your life

have an incredible outlook
and you'll have an incredible life

IF YOU DON'T KNOW

If you don't know who you are
then you won't know what you need

if you don't know what you need
cultural society will influence
you into becoming somebody
you were never meant to be

drifting so far from yourself
that it takes radical change
for you to find your way back home

WE USE OUR AWARENESS

We use our awareness
in different ways

some ignore it
some focus on positive awareness
some focus on negative awareness

some don't want to meet it at all
some can't live without it

some know it and nothing changes
some know it and everything changes

some learn it
some want it so desperately and don't get it

some of us close our eyes
and can only see darkness

but some of us close our eyes
and can see the whole universe

THE WAR INSIDE

To bring peace to the war outside
we have to first heal the war inside

the harder the burn
the deeper the wound

and it's been
generations

PLANES OF OUR PLANETS

It is only the construct of our conditioning
that keeps us imprisoned

freedom is when you let go
of everything you think you know
everything you think you are

and for a moment
you are nobody

nothing but a spark of light
dancing on the planes of our planets

unable to fit into any stereotype
simply because the concept just doesn't exist

only existence exists
evoking, evolving and then evaporating

give yourself a clean slate
because if you want to see change

you must first become it

THE CLOUDS OF HEAVEN

Even the highest peak
of the tallest mountain

has taken it's time
to reach the clouds of heaven

you are not exempt
allow your process to gracefully unfold

BE YOURSELF

There is no greater pain
than not loving yourself

not feeling yourself
not hearing yourself
not seeing yourself

for the love of god
be yourself

Chemistry Of Our Love
And Discrepancies

There's you
one entity

and then there's me
a separate entity

when we are together
we are combined energy

the value of our chemistry
increases with love

and decreases with
negative discrepancies

It Takes You

We are on the front lines
of an invisible revolution

you can feel it in the air
you can see it in the people

it can be a massive movement
or a subtle energy shift

but we are waking up
from a deathly slumber

it doesn't take two
it takes you

WHOLENESS

Eat food that's had a good life

that has been kissed by the rain
and warmed by the sun

that's free to breathe
and feel the wind

allow yourself to experience edible wholeness
our cells regenerate

what we eat
is what we become

to work with food is primal
it connects us back to basic survival

One Person At A Time

You either want the knowledge
or you don't

you're either committed to healing
or you've not

once you've looked deeply into your own soul
you see we are all one in the same

and you can finally understand
that the struggle of the individual
effects the whole

that healing of the individual
get's us closer to healing the whole
one person at a time

A Reason To Start

if you're searching for a reason to start
there might not be one

you have to want it
without reason

want it for you
want to sweat through it

want to cry for it
want to watch it grow

want to feel it take form
and see it take flight

if you want it
look where you're going
because that's where you're headed

Paula

....

Physical distance
does not separate the closeness of hearts
you are always with me

I can always feel you
I can always hear you
and I will always love you

To Prolong Life

We are programmed to prolong life
but in the most
ridiculous, dangerous way

not something simple
such as elongating the breath
breathing life into ourselves

we are prolonging the way we look
over prolonging the way we live

I HAVE BEEN

I have been conned
I have been crooked

I have been dead around the living
I have been alive around the dead

I have been homesick
I have been lovesick
I have been guilt-sick

I have hurt people
I have hurt myself

I have felt lost within myself
I have felt lonely in a room full of people

I have sang songs of heartache
I have climbed mountains bloodied and
torn apart

I have been bruised and beaten
I have abused myself and been used by others

I have cried myself to sleep too many times
to count
I have flown miles across the world
to find love

I have worked until exhaustion
I have danced until i couldn't stand
I have wept until i couldn't breathe

I have seen what hate can do
I have seen what love can do
I have seen what god can do

because of that
I have everything to gain
and nothing to lose

QUANTITY OF BALANCE

Love and fear become the same thing
when we talk about them in quantity

too little love leads to being
emotionally stunted
too much love leads to compulsive obsession

too much fear leads to paralysis
too little fear leads to playing with fire

when it comes to more or less
let balance be the guide

LET IT POUR OUT OF YOU

Do not cling to love
let it pour out of you

do not cling to fame
let it find you

do not cling to being heard
let your action speak for itself

do not cling to existence
let life be one of many journeys

do not cling to an outcome
let yourself be astonished

do not cling to anything
not even the idea of who you are

WE ARE WHAT WE BELIEVE

. . . .

Never underestimate
the potential of a powerful mantra

we are what we believe we are

Shadows And Old Spirits

....

If you hold fear within memories
and anxiety within thoughts

remember the shadows can seem bigger
and scarier in your mind

sometimes all you need to do
is talk about what's happened to you

so you are able to confront
the old spirits
and bid them farewell

LIVING IN COLOR

Have the strength
to admit when you've wrong

to cry when you've hurting
to shout when you've angry

have the freedom
to let yourself laugh
and celebrate your milestones

have the power to feel everything
rather than nothing

to be hopelessly and radiantly alive
than painfully numb

some might choose to live their lives in
black and white
but you can choose to live yours in color

Honor The Adjustment

All you have to do
is wake up

see through it
past it
beyond it

and everything else
will rise in perfect alignment
to honor the adjustment

SILENCE

You find silence
as a response

when you keep
being left speechless

BE RAW

Be raw
but know what you say
gets carried in the wind

life is full of what you didn't do
where you didn't go

but its made up of
what you did do
where you did go

what you will do
where you will go

you can travel far and wide
but if you don't journey inside
the distance doesn't matter

CALLED FORWARD

You're being called forward

called on to look
listen and learn

called on to respond
reevaluate and restore yourself

called on to integrate
resuscitate and activate

GETTING BETTER

The sweeter you are to your mind
the kinder you are to your body
and the healthier your thoughts become

if you don't put effort into getting better
you'll remain ill

if you can't physically move
exercise your mind

if you can't use your mind
exercise your body

REACH FOR THE GOLD

The body is a powerful machine
but powerless without a strong mind to direct it

you're going to have to work
there's no question

it's going to take guts, tears
and sleepless nights

it's going to feel like deep loss
followed by tremendous gain

it's going to break you
wide open

you'll fail before you succeed
you'll succeed before you fail

it's going to be the most challenging thing
you've embarked on yet

but the outcome will be otherworldly
something you only could have imagined
in your wildest dreams

don't look back
reach for the gold
with everything you've got

Afterword

You have to become less of yourself to
embody more of the self. Which is of course
formless but visible to the curious of hearts.
Go courageously on your voyage to the other
side of discovering who you really are.

S.P.